Suburban Classic

NEW YORK CITY'S NEIGHBORS & THEIR PEOPLE

Patrick Jackson

Schiffer Publishing Ltd

4880 Lower Valley Road • Atglen, PA 19310

This book is dedicated to my wonderful parents,

Mark and Francine Jackson

Published by Schiffer Publishing, Ltd.
4880 Lower Valley Road
Atglen, PA 19310
Phone: (610) 593-1777; Fax: (610) 593-2002
E-mail: Info@schifferbooks.com

For our complete selection of fine books on this and related subjects, please visit our website at www.schifferbooks.com. You may also write for a free catalog.

This book may be purchased from the publisher. Please try your bookstore first.

We are always looking for people to write books on new and related subjects. If you have an idea for a book, please contact us at proposals@schifferbooks.com

Schiffer Publishing's titles are available at special discounts for bulk purchases for sales promotions or premiums. Special editions, including personalized covers, corporate imprints, and excerpts can be created in large quantities for special needs. For more information, contact the publisher.

CONTENTS

FOREWORD

Growing up in upstate New York, the first chance I got, I took off for New York City. I wanted the action, the excitement, and the endless opportunity of big city living. I was chasing my small town dreams and, until I arrived in downtown New York, wandering around the village, it felt like nowhere was big enough to hold them.

My love for New York continues, but today the escape to the open landscapes and big skies of quaint suburbs around New York brings a happy harmony to city living. Relaxation, quality family time and nature's great expanse all feel a little more readily available in the villages, hamlets and towns of Connecticut, Long Island, northern New Jersey, and upstate New York. I have always loved the striking architecture and the requisite main streets of the small historical towns of the Northeast. A drive through these picturesque neighborhoods reveals a special sort of living – quiet, calm and quite distinct from their big city counterpart.

One of the best parts about New England living is the ease of finding a balance between the two extremes. With storied summer retreats turning into thriving year-round communities, there's all the sudden access to the quintessential suburban lifestyle almost in the heart of the city!

The delicate and beautiful equilibrium of American small town living amidst one of the great cultural capitals of the world has never been better explored than in these pages.

Tommy Hilfiger

Tommy Hilfiger

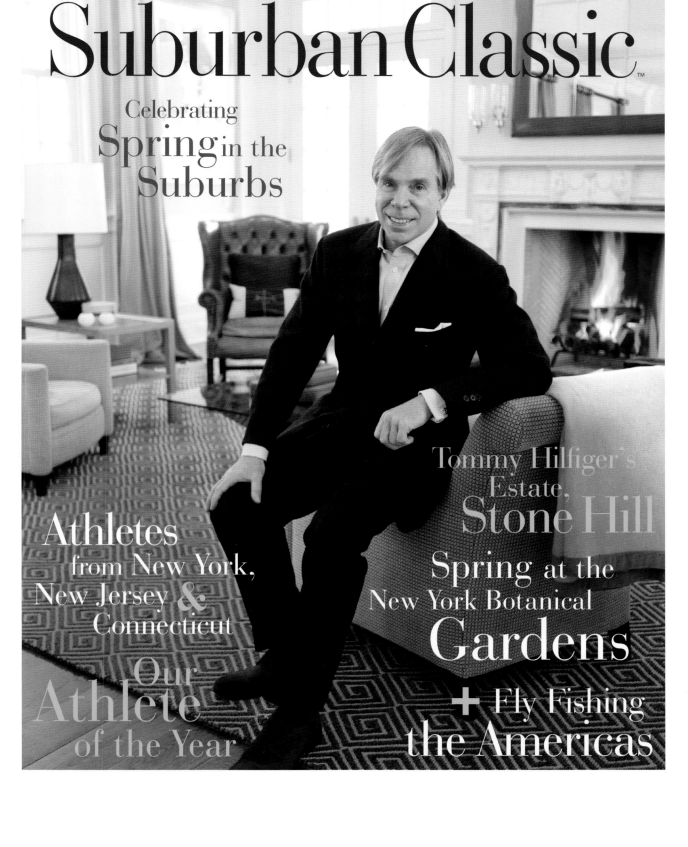

Suburban Classic™

Celebrating
Spring in the
Suburbs

Athletes
from New York,
New Jersey &
Connecticut

Our
Athlete
of the Year

Tommy Hilfiger's
Estate,
Stone Hill

Spring at the
New York Botanical
Gardens

+ Fly Fishing
the Americas

INTRODUCTION

Patrick with his nephew, John Kemp Jackson

New York City is considered by many to be the greatest city in the world. The energy, commerce, and excitement generated by the Big Apple are unparalleled. The suburbs that surround the city are home to many of the movers and shakers that make Manhattan sparkle. These bedroom communities that New York commuters call home are in Connecticut, New York, and New Jersey, and are as special in their exquisite beauty and style as New York City itself.

From 2005 through 2010, I tried to capture the aura of this metropolis in a magazine called *Suburban Classic*. The magazine was a long overdue tribute to the greatest suburban area anywhere in the United States. The magazine quickly developed a loyal following and was in fact the inspiration for this book.

The suburbia we feature in this book encompasses three states and five million people, including some of the most interesting, unique families and communities in the country. Our focus is on suburban life in this special corner of the world. This book is a collection of some of our best work over the past ten years, much of which has never been published before.

Patrick F. Jackson

NEW YORK BOTANICAL GARDEN

BRONX, NEW YORK

The New York Botanical Garden is unique among museums and public places in America and is distinguished by the beauty of its historic landscapes, collections, and gardens. The New York Botanical Garden is one of the world's great collections of plants, the region's leading educational center for gardening and horticulture, and an international center of plant science. And, incredibly, the New York Botanical Garden is less than twenty minutes from midtown Manhattan.

As a living museum of plants and a leader in horticulture excellence, the Botanical Garden features 50 magnificent gardens and plant collections across 250 beautiful acres and is home to dozens of horticultural events, such as The Orchid Show.

A national historic landmark, the Botanical Garden is also home to the nation's largest Victorian-style glasshouse, the Enid A. Haupt Conservatory, itself a New York City landmark. The Conservatory's permanent exhibition, A World of Plants, includes tropical rainforests, deserts, and the world's most comprehensive collection of New World palm trees under glass.

ARMONK

NEW YORK

Tucked away in the northeastern section of Westchester County, New York, is Armonk, a hamlet within the town of North Castle. Located approximately 35 miles from midtown Manhattan, Armonk's unique location is often credited with being a primary reason for moving into this beautiful community. Locals can take the train into New York City in less than 40 minutes, drive into downtown Greenwich, Connecticut, in 15 minutes, or zip over to the Westchester Airport or the city of White Plains, New York, in just 10 minutes.

An outstanding school district, a quaint downtown shopping district with some of Westchester's best restaurants, several private clubs, and charming neighborhoods situated among heavily wooded forests and sparkling lakes also help make Armonk an ideal place to live.

The town has always been noted for its natural beauty and the recent addition of the Mariani Garden Center has been received with a warm welcome. The stunning, four-acre garden center opened to rave reviews in 2006 and has become one of the area's most popular destinations. The garden center has state-of-the-art greenhouses, a luxury home décor center, an exclusive floral department, an extraordinary selection of rare and unusual trees and shrubs, as well as its own café, which is a perfect place for Sunday Brunch or a weekday snack.

SCARSDALE

NEW YORK

Scarsdale is an upscale community in Westchester County, New York, located 24 miles north of Manhattan. The town is particularly well known for having an outstanding school district, including one of the top public high schools in the nation. Ninety-nine percent of the students graduate and go on to higher education, many being accepted to the nation's most prestigious colleges and universities.

First-time visitors will surely be impressed with the elegant Tudor-style buildings seen throughout the downtown village center. The town itself is surrounded by several well-maintained parks that enhance the overall atmosphere of an old fashioned shopping district reminiscent of years past.

While driving through many of the neighborhoods, you will be pleasantly surprised to see how many original homes still remain. Fortunately, most residents have chosen to preserve and restore these landmark homes, as opposed to replacing them with larger but less attractive colossuses.

Beautiful neighborhoods, an exquisite shopping district, a top-notch public school system, and a close proximity to New York City make Scarsdale an ideal place to live and raise a family.

Finally, one very interesting observation one will make while visiting or driving through Scarsdale is that there is a very large population of all-black squirrels, which exist no where else in the area.

LARCHMONT

NEW YORK

There is a memorable scene in the film *Wall Street,* where the main character, Gordon Gekko, is in the changing room of a prestigious men's health club and he asks another member, "How's Larchmont treating you?" After personally visiting for a photoshoot, it certainly appears that Larchmont happens to be treating its residents very well.

Larchmont is a small, affluent village located within the town of Mamaroneck, on the shore of the Long Island Sound in Westchester County, New York. It has a population of about 7,000 residents.

Larchmont and several of the neighboring towns have long been noted for their significant French-American populous, and thus it is not surprising that the prestigious French-American School of New York is located in the village of Larchmont.

Despite its small size, Larchmont certainly has a lot to offer residents: great schools, an exceptional downtown shopping area, excellent restaurants, manicured parks, several noted private clubs, and beautiful beaches. Best of all, it is located less than 20 miles from New York City, making Larchmont one of the most commuter-friendly suburbs in the New York City tristate area.

If you're visiting Larchmont for the first time, make sure to take a drive through the historic "Manor Park" section of the village. The old-fashioned homes, well-maintained gardens, and lovely views provided by the Long Island Sound have made these neighborhoods some of the most desirable places to live in all of Westchester County.

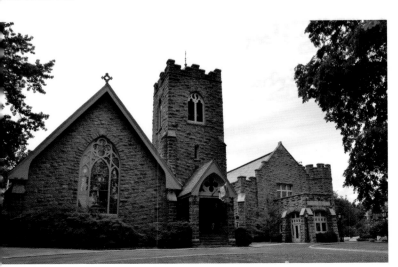

RYE

NEW YORK

Rye is a picturesque town in Westchester County, New York, located on the Long Island Sound. It has a population of approximately 46,000 and has long been considered one of the most desirable places to live in Westchester County.

Magnificent homes and estates, as well as some of the most spectacular private yacht clubs on the East Coast, have helped cement Rye's reputation as one of the most exclusive waterfront communities in the country.

However, for many residents, the primary reason for living in Rye is that the town provides a truly exceptional experience for their children. Besides having a top-notch school system, the appeal for many parents is the incredible variety of extracurricular activities available. The town has multiple recreational facilities, including manicured athletic fields, lighted basketball courts,

volleyball courts, tennis courts, picnic areas, playgrounds, and even a skate park. The town also has a YMCA, conveniently located in the center of town, that offers numerous programs to children of all ages.

The Rye Nature Center is another town feature popular with both parents and their children. Both the YMCA and the Nature Center provide a wide variety of educational programs for children.

Additionally, it is nice having an amusement park right in your own backyard. Rye Playland is a historic amusement park that was built in 1928. Wildly popular with both kids and adults, the amusement park is just another added bonus to a kid-friendly town that seems to have it all.

Manursing Island Club

A special thanks to photographer Valerie Donohue for providing us with these incredible wildlife images, that were all taken at the Rye Marshlands Conservancy

BEDFORD

NEW YORK

While driving though the town of Bedford, it is hard to believe that you are only 43 miles away from New York City. Located in Westchester County, New York, Bedford is one of the most affluent communities in the country.

Designed after a traditional New England village in 1680, the town really hasn't changed much over the years. Stunning country estates, rolling hills, horse farms, winding roads, and rustic stonewalls are all part of what makes Bedford such a visually beautiful, old-fashioned community.

Although Bedford is still occasionally referred to as a farming community, today it is more commonly described as a horse town, as many of its residents belong to the Bedford Riding Lanes Association. For a small annual membership fee, residents are given access to over 200 miles of the best riding trails on the East Coast.

The town of Bedford is not only popular with horse lovers, it also happens to be very popular with many celebrities. Ralph Lauren, Martha Stewart, Richard Gere, and Michael Douglas are just a few who call Bedford home.

The Bedford Oak is the town's most fascinating landmark. The enormous tree is believed to be over 300 years old, with moss-covered branches that span over 130 feet across.

If you have never driven through the town of Bedford, make a point to visit. You will not be disappointed!

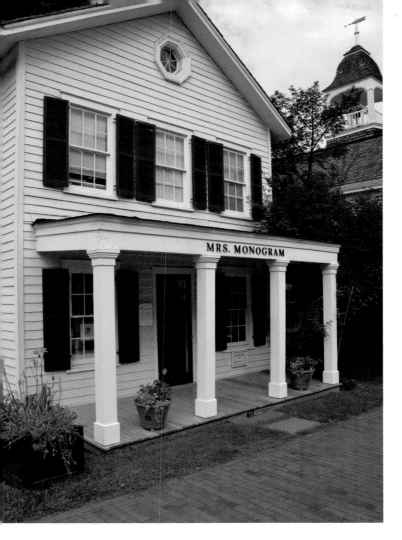

CHAPPAQUA

NEW YORK

Chappaqua is a hamlet in northern Westchester County, located in the town of Newcastle, New York. It has the small-town feel of a quaint New England village and is located just 35 miles from New York City, just 45 minutes by train and about an hour by car.

As with most communities in the county, it boasts great schools, beautiful homes, extensive sports programs for children, and downtown shopping and dining.

Just outside the downtown area, the surroundings unexpectedly change to a pristine, untouched, natural wilderness with marshland, open fields, lakes, and towering evergreens. Local conservationists have insured that Chappaqua will forever be eco-friendly, with multiple town parks and the 300-acre Sawmill Audubon Society County Park, located in its environs.

As with its tony counterparts, Chappaqua also has its own celebrities, Bill and Hillary Clinton, who can often be seen walking their dog and enjoying this wonderful village.

KATONAH

NEW YORK

People who live in Katonah often refer to their community as a village, however Katonah is actually one of three unincorporated hamlets within the town of Bedford, which is located in Westchester County, New York.

Katonah has an old-fashioned downtown shopping district with several restaurants, cafes, art galleries, and the well-known Katonah Public Library. On the outskirts of the downtown center are numerous turn-of-the-century Victorian homes and a stunning white Victorian church.

There is an abundance of recreational activities that are available to both residents and the general public. One place certainly worth visiting would be the John Jay Homestead, the former home of the first Chief Justice of the Supreme Court of the United States. The well-preserved, federal-style home and the extensive gardens surrounding the residence are now a state historic site.

To say that residents of this relatively small community celebrate the arts would be an understatement. The Katonah Museum of Art hosts numerous exhibitions throughout the year, featuring contemporary painting, sculpture, and photography. The museum also has an interesting outdoor sculpture garden. The Katonah Historical Museum celebrates the community's unique past. Music lovers will certainly enjoy the Caramoor International Music Festival. The Festival takes place at the Caramoor Estates, and is generally regarded as one of the top outdoor music festivals in the nation, featuring some of the world's finest classical, operatic, and jazz artists.

THE CRANBERRY LAKE PRESERVE

WHITE PLAINS, NEW YORK

The sign at the entrance of the Cranberry Lake Preserve is a reminder to visitors that they are in an incredibly important place!

The 190-acre park operated by the Westchester County Department of Parks, Recreation and Conservation is indeed special. The well-maintained hiking trails lead visitors through a variety of habitats including a four-acre lake, dense scrubland, mixed hardwood forest, vernal pools, a swamp and the ever-popular Rock Quarry. The Rock Quarry, which is surrounded by steep cliffs, provides visitors with some awe-inspiring views. Don't forget to bring your camera!

The park has been a safe haven for animals and plants since 1967. Visitors who arrive early before the park gets crowded, may be surprised by how many different animals they encounter during their hike. Some commonly seen wildlife includes turkey vultures, hawks, painted turtles, chipmunks, black rat snakes, frogs, and toads.

However, it is some of the rarer species that draw photographers and avid wildlife enthusiasts. Although in decline and becoming increasingly rare due to over-collecting, which is highly illegal, both the Spotted Turtle and Eastern Box Turtle can be seen occasionally at the park. Bald Eagles and Osprey have also been known to visit the park and just recently there has been a confirmed sighting of a bobcat.

In addition, the preserve is fortunate to have a very small deer population, which has been very beneficial to the wide variety of plant life found throughout the park. Wildflowers, ferns, water lilies, colorful mushrooms of all shapes and sizes, and three known variety of orchids can all be found at the Cranberry Lake Preserve.

Located on the border of West Harrison and North White Plains, New York, the park is a hidden gem. Whether you're into trail running, photography, bird watching, or just getting outside to enjoy nature, a trip to the Cranberry Lake Preserve is always a rewarding experience.

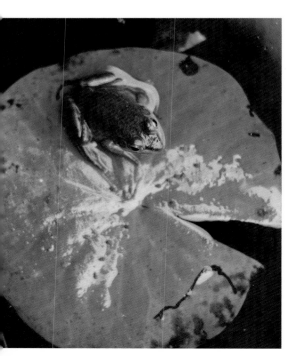

YOU ARE IN AN INCREDIBLY
IMPORTANT PLACE!

Cranberry Lake Preserve
BIODIVERSITY RESERVE AREA

Please help us take care of this unique place

- Take nothing but memories. All plants, animals, and minerals are protected.
- Please keep dogs and bikes at home.
- Fishing is prohibited.
- Stay on designated hiking trails.
- Carry out what you carry in.
- Visit Nature Center with comments.

Thank you for your patronage – Enjoy your visit!

P★RKS
WESTCHESTER COUNTY

OLD WESTBURY GARDENS

OLD WESTBURY, NEW YORK

Old Westbury Gardens was the home of John Shaffer Phipps, one of the heirs of the U.S. Steel fortune. The 200-acre estate began in 1903 and was completed in 1906. The grounds of the estate were inspired by Phipps's English wife, Margarita Grace, and are styled as traditional, formal English Gardens, which include rose gardens, walled courtyard gardens, ponds, lakes, arbors, statuary, and fountains, all connected by intricate hedged walkways that flow into large landscaped grounds. These gardens are only rivaled by Versailles, home of French King Louis XVI and his wife Marie Antoinette.

On the estate is also the impeccable 70-room Charles II-style mansion, which still contains many of the antique furnishings and timeless paintings that originally graced this massive family home. This magnificent turn-of-the-century, Gold Coast fairyland has been open to the public for over 50 years. It is only 20 miles east of New York City and it is a look into a pampered lifestyle of a golden age, even rivalling the living arrangements of our wealthiest tycoons today.

CENTRE ISLAND

NEW YORK

Long Island's North Shore, an area often referred to as the Gold Coast, is home to some of the wealthiest and most prestigious communities in the United States.

Perhaps the region's most exclusive section is a 605-acre peninsula known as Centre Island. The Village of Centre Island is an ultra-private community located within the town of Oyster Bay in Nassau County, New York. Surprisingly, the village has no shopping district and remains largely undeveloped, much to the delight of its residents. The only structures are the 200 or so homes, the magnificent yacht club, and the small police station at the entrance of Centre Island.

The tidal creeks, grassy marshlands, several heavily wooded areas, and four miles of sandy beaches have all contributed to giving the village the unique atmosphere of a nature sanctuary.

Centre Island has been a popular retreat for the rich and famous for many years. The village is noted for magnificent waterfront estates, spectacular views, and several celebrity residents including musician Billy Joel. Curiously, there are actually several smaller homes built on half-acre lots scattered throughout the village. Some of these homes occasionally come on the market, providing an opportunity to move into one of the most spectacular private communities at a very reasonable price. So keep your eye open for the bargain of a lifetime.

MANHASSET

NEW YORK

Manhasset is a 2.5 square-mile hamlet, a short train ride away from Manhattan. Its name comes from a Native American term meaning island neighborhood, and it may be the premier neighborhood in all of Nassau County, Long Island. This tony town, with about 8,000 residents, has great schools, great high school sports teams, and maybe the nicest shopping area east of Rodeo Drive in Beverly Hills, California, or north of Worth Avenue in Palm Beach, Florida. That shopping area, dominated by the open-air Americana Manhasset, is known as the Miracle Mile, and was referenced in Billy Joel's classic song "It's Still Rock and Roll to Me." If you are moving anywhere in Nassau County, you want to live in or near to Manhasset.

How nice is Manhasset? Well the *Wall Street Journal* picked it as the best town for raising a family in the New York Metropolitan area in 2005. Even the lawyer, who marries Maureen O'Hara and becomes dad to young Natalie Wood in the Christmas classic *Miracle on 34th Street*, confides to Kris Kringle that he would like to buy a nice Colonial home in Manhasset. What greater endorsement could anyone want?

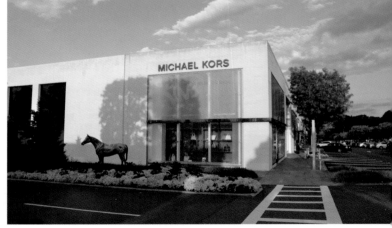

SOUTHAMPTON

NEW YORK

Some of the most beautiful towns and beaches in the world are located in an area referred to as the Hamptons. The Hamptons consist of a large stretch of picturesque coastal communities approximately 100 miles east of New York City. The most exclusive enclave of the Hamptons has always been Southampton, a tiny village of less than 4,000 people. Today, Southampton has become one of the most desirable summer destinations for New York's entertainment community, as well as anyone who has made a small fortune on Wall Street, media, fashion, or real estate. Nevertheless, the crowd in Southampton is, surprisingly, very diverse. Celebrities, socialites, and Wall Street titans make up only a small part of the population. Southampton is also home to many artists, surfers, writers, athletes, and a large number of Native Americans.

What makes Southampton one of the world's greatest summer retreats is its accessibility by car, rail, and air, and its location near Midtown Manhattan. Furthermore, Southampton has one of the best beaches in the county, Coopers Beach,

according to the 2008 Review of America's Best 100 Beaches.

Southampton also has the most complete shopping area in the Hamptons, along with its own version of Rodeo Drive, referred to as Jobs Lane and dating back to the mid-1600s. In addition, the town has the only hospital on the east end, Southampton Hospital, where Jackie Kennedy was born. This hospital hosts one of the greatest fundraising parties of the summer season.

In town, you could easily eat in a different restaurant every day of the summer and not have a repeat visit, but favorites seem to be Shippy's, for the best food, 75 Main Street, which serves classic American cuisine, or the more egalitarian Driver's Seat, which is always packed and fun.

The neighborhoods, homes, and gardens throughout Southampton are so magnificent that words do not give them justice. If that's not enough, wait until you get a chance to experience the nightlife. During July and August the nightlife in Southampton is simply sensational and the people-watching is second to none.

Munn Point

SOUTHAMPTON, NEW YORK

The Munn Point land preserve is a pristine nature sanctuary and an ideal place to observe wildlife. One day, while visiting the village of Southampton, I drove to the park to take a few test shots with a camera I had just purchased. Walking toward the water, I overheard a young girl ask her grandmother "was the sanctuary really named after Grandpa?" The grandmother responded, "Yes it is!" I turned to the grandmother and asked her the same question. To my surprise, she confirmed that the Munn Point was in fact named after her husband. She also told me he was in his car nearby and asked if I would like to meet him. Of course I wanted to meet her husband and got them to agree to an impromptu photo shoot. This photo of Orson Munn, his wife and granddaughter was taken in late spring of 2008 and appeared in our Summer 2008 issue.

BRIDGEHAMPTON POLO

BRIDGEHAMPTON, NEW YORK

The Hamptons has always been the playground for the rich and famous, and during the summer the number of exciting events that occur there are virtually limitless.

Perhaps the most spectacular of all events that are open to the public are the Saturday afternoon polo matches held in Bridgehampton. With countless A-list celebrities and many of the East End's high-profile socialites in attendance on a regular basis, the polo matches are, without question, the best place for people watching in the Hamptons. The actual sporting event is also truly great entertainment, as spectators are given an opportunity to watch some of the world's greatest equestrian

athletes participate in highly competitive polo matches. First time visitors will certainly enjoy the "half-time show" as spectators go on to the field in a social tradition called "divot stomping." Guests literally help to temporarily patch up the field, while mingling, sipping champagne and enjoying the beautiful landscape.

If you have heard great things about the Bridgehampton Polo Matches, they are all true. The friendly atmosphere, the well-dressed crowd, and the affordable admission fee make this event a terrific way to spend your afternoon in the Hamptons.

MONTAUK

NEW YORK

Not too long ago, Montauk was little more than a small, quiet, fishing village located at the tip of Long Island. Blessed with a great deal of natural beauty and some of the world's most spectacular beaches, it was only a matter of time before word spread that Montauk was a great summer destination.

Today, Montauk has become one of the most popular and storied beach resorts on the East Coast. A thriving nightlife, quaint downtown shopping district, great places to surf, including Ditch Plains Beach, affordable lodging, and a casual, laid back atmosphere are what visitors and residents find so appealing about this unique town.

Fishing is also just as popular as ever, and Montauk's reputation among anglers for being an exceptional destination is well deserved. Numerous world records for saltwater fishing have been set off the coast of Montauk, most notably a 3,427-pound Great White Shark. Legendary fisherman and local legend Frank Mundas, the inspiration for the "tough as nails" shark hunter Quint in the film *Jaws,* captured the beast in 1986 and it is believed to be the largest shark ever caught with a rod and reel.

Although Montauk has grown, it still maintains much of its original charm. By setting aside over 5,000 acres of pristine wilderness and leaving beautiful beaches untouched, the town fathers have guaranteed that future generations will be able to enjoy this special section of the Hamptons, which fortunately will always remain underdeveloped.

GREENWICH

CONNECTICUT

Greenwich, Connecticut, has a reputation for being one of the most desirable places to live in the world. Located in Fairfield County, Connecticut, and less than thirty miles from Manhattan, Greenwich offers its residents a dizzying array of amenities.

With over sixty thousand residents, the town is actually larger than many people would assume. Within the town of Greenwich there are seven separate villages; Old Greenwich, Cos Cob, Riverside, Byram, Central Greenwich, Glenville, and Banksville.

A world-renowned shopping district, fine dining, a sensational public library, a public golf course, the Greenwich Polo Club, and an outstanding school system are just a few of the reasons why Greenwich has always ranked among the most desirable places to live.

The natural beauty of Greenwich is another major draw. With over thirty miles of shoreline on the Long Island Sound, the town has several public beaches where residents unwind and relax.

The areas further away from the beach are commonly referred to as "mid-country" and "back country," and are equally beautiful. Grand estates, built among the rolling hills and pristine wildernesses of Greenwich, are a common sight in the back country. The town has done a remarkable job of not overdeveloping the land, and has over 8000 acres of protected land, including 1500 acres of parkland, which are open to the public.

Another popular feature that Greenwich provides its residents is one of the lowest property tax rates in the state of Connecticut.

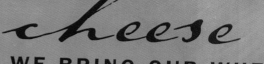

WE BRING OUR WHEELS T

Backyard Beautiful– Mariani Style

GREEENWICH, CONNECTICUT

Mark Mariani is a successful and sought-after builder, who has become well known over the years for designing, building, and completing 20,000 square foot homes in as little as six months.

One high profile project that received a great deal of media attention and fully illustrates Mariani's unique talent was the spectacular custom home he built for the popular celebrity, Judge Judy. In order to complete the job in just 80 days, his men worked around the clock. Sometimes there were as many as 500 workers on the building site at once. This particular home could be more accurately described as an estate. The main house was an 18,000 square foot masterpiece. Included on the property is a guesthouse, guardhouse, pool house, formal gardens, and a pool. To complete the project, Mariani created a landscape that appears to have been there for years, by planting mature trees and bushes sourced from his many private tree and boxwood farms.

In addition to being a successful builder, Mariani is also one of the most talented landscape designers in the area. His name is synonymous with gardening excellence and has been for some time. For years Mark Mariani has created stunning landscapes and gardens for the rich and famous in and around Fairfield and Westchester counties.

If you assumed that the area's premiere landscape designer had a beautiful backyard himself, you would be correct. Over the years, we had heard from people who had seen the yard on the Greenwich Garden tour that the Mariani backyard was magnificent. So we stopped by the Mariani's beautiful garden center in Armonk, New York, and asked if we could include a few photos of the yard in our book. We were thrilled when he agreed and invited us over to do a photo shoot. Not only did we manage to get some great shots for this layout, but we also got the perfect cover shot.

ROWAYTON

CONNECTICUT

Painters, photographers, and architects have long been inspired by the natural beauty of the quaint, New England-style, seaside village called Rowayton. Located within the city of Norwalk, Connecticut, the most obvious attraction of this affluent, beautiful community is that no matter where you are in Rowayton, you are either on the water, near the water, or right down the street from the water. Beautiful beaches, tidal creeks, and water views provided by Long Island Sound and the Five Mile River have given its residents a laid-back, beach town feel unlike any other community in Connecticut.

Those who enjoy sailing, fishing, paddle boarding, kayaking, clamming, or just lounging at the beach and who are looking for a little bit of Nantucket in Fairfield County, Connecticut, will find Rowayton to be a dream town. Many of the 4,000 residents share the common belief that, if you live in Rowayton, there is certainly no need to ever purchase a summer home. After all, summer in Rowayton happens to be as good as it gets!

DARIEN

CONNECTICUT

Darien is a lovely town in Fairfield County, Connecticut, with a population of approximately 20,000 people. Situated between the small cities of Norwalk and Stamford and located only 38 miles away from Manhattan, it is a charming bedroom community and an ideal place to raise a family.

Families who move to Darien experience exquisite neighborhoods, beautiful public beaches, and a staggering number of recreational activities that are available.

Parents will be thrilled with the competitive youth athletics and the number of high caliber sports clinics and leagues offered each season. The town enjoys a well-deserved reputation for producing terrific young athletes in many different sports, and is particularly well known for their varsity lacrosse teams. As the sport of lacrosse continues to grow in popularity, Darien High School remains the team to beat in Connecticut. The state lacrosse tournament is often referred to as "The Darien Invitational." Both the boys and girls varsity lacrosse teams are now recognized nationally as some of the country's best programs.

Darien's impressive athletic facilities, which include an equestrian center, a baseball park, a spectacular indoor skating rink, and multiple manicured playing fields, are all testament to the town's passion for sports.

While in Darien, athletes and shoppers of all ages will enjoy a visit to the Darien Sport Shop. This store has been the area's most popular destination for over seven decades and it is much more than simply a place to buy tennis shoes. This family-owned business is the Harrods of Darien. It is also well known for promoting community pride. Nearly all the walls on the first floor of the shop are covered with local artists' paintings and photographs. Upstairs in the sports department, local teams and athletes who have been featured in newspapers and regional magazines are prominently displayed.

DARIEN SPORT SHOP INC.
EST. 1946
STEPHEN F. ZANGRILLO, SR.

NEW CANAAN

CONNECTICUT

New Canaan is as beautiful a town as one will ever encounter in the North East. While it is technically not in New England, it certainly has that feel about it. The downtown looks like Hometown, USA, and, because of that, it has been used for location scenes in many movies and television shows. When Author Garrison Keillor described the fictional Lake Wobegon as "the little town that time forgot, and decades cannot improve. A town where all the women are strong, and the men are good looking, and all the children are above average," he came pretty close to describing New Caanan. It is a town where high achievers move to raise their families. And being just 45 miles from New York, and being served by the Metro North railroad,

it is an easy commute to New York City. New Canaan is home to CEOs, actors and actresses, architects, and owners of billion dollar companies. The population has doubled every 50 years or so since the early 1800s and stands, now, at a population of about 20,000. The town is about 22.5 square miles in area, so there is still room to grow. It also was ground zero for the modern design movement in residential architecture and, from the late 1940s to the early 1960s, 80 homes were designed by the "Harvard Five." It is a town that calls for the use of superlatives when describing it, and a town that residents, and those that long to be residents, love to love.

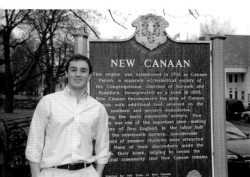

WESTPORT

CONNECTICUT

A delightful suburban community, Westport has much to offer its residents. Situated on the coast of Fairfield County, Connecticut, it is known for its history and stunningly beautiful neighborhoods. With a touch of rural charm and spectacular views of Long Island Sound, the town combines the perks of a suburban setting with easy access to New York City.

Recognized as one of the most affluent communities in the United States, Westport is located on Long Island Sound and the Saugatuck River. The town features an array of fine restaurants, entertainment venues, and sports facilities including equestrian, yacht, and golf clubs.

When residents aren't relaxing at the beach, they spend much of their time enjoying free entertainment at the Levitt Pavilion. The venue showcases impressive talent in a series of outdoor performances. Also noteworthy are the other performing arts centers, such as the Westport Country Playhouse and Westport Art Center. As a town with a strong history and appreciation for artists and actors, Westport is a breeding ground for success in the arts.

Westport has a large number of celebrity residents, leading many locals to refer to the town as "Hollywood East." The populace studiously ignores the better-known residents, resulting in many of the famous personalities believing that Westport is an ideal place to duck their celebrity. Clearly, it's a great place to be treated like anyone else.

If you haven't experienced this great treat of a town, by all means do so. You never can tell whom you will see or what town-sponsored event you may stumble upon, but one thing is sure, every day in Westport is a memorable one.

SOUTHPORT

CONNECTICUT

Southport is an extremely affluent and exclusive section of Fairfield, Connecticut. Located approximately 50 miles from New York City, the quiet village of Southport has, for many years, been a desirable place to live for the rich and famous, especially those who love sailing and golf. This lovely community is one of the most picturesque coastal villages in the country. It is well known for its historical district along the harbor, which provides commanding views over the Country Club of Fairfield, and the Long Island Sound.

First time visitors will surely be impressed with the attention to detail and overall craftsmanship that is apparent in Southport's diverse architecture. The magnificent antique homes seen throughout the historical district have a grandeur, class, and sheer beauty that are nearly matchless.

Southport also has a charming downtown shopping district, several private clubs, including the exquisite Pequot Yacht Club, great restaurants, beautiful public beaches, and an exceptional sports and recreation facility at the Wakeman Boys and Girls Club. The village of Southport is truly an amazing place to live and a great place to visit, especially from May through October, when the weather is most ideal.

If you are looking for an ideal weekend getaway, think about staying at Southport's luxurious Delamar Hotel and explore this wonderful community for yourself. Don't forget to bring your bathing suit and a camera.

RIDGEWOOD

NEW JERSEY

It's not a coincidence that many people who grew up in Ridgewood, New Jersey, eventually wind up moving back to raise their families.

Ridgewood happens to be one of the most livable villages in any of New York City's suburbs.

The village offers easy access into Manhattan by train, bus, or car, which is critical because most of the town's professionals commute into the city for work. It also has one of the model school systems in the state of New Jersey. Ridgewood schools always rate high in national polls.

With a large shopping district, offering dozens of restaurants, a movie theater, and tony boutiques, Ridgewood draws residents from many surrounding towns. They enjoy the great shopping and nightlife in a central downtown area that resembles a Norman Rockwell painting or an antique postcard depicting an old-fashioned village shopping district.

It has often been said that there is no need to leave Ridgewood for anything, as it has its own hospital, library, and town swimming hole. The village also has several popular events that occur each year, some drawing as many as 10,000 spectators. The Fourth of July Parade, the Ridgewood Run, the Thanksgiving Day football game, and Ridgewood Lacrosse Day provide truly exceptional entertainment for the townsfolk, and they are all open to the public. So make a point to visit Ridgewood sometime and spend the day exploring this wonderful village for yourself.

HO-HO-KUS

NEW JERSEY

Ho-Ho-Kus is a tiny town, with a funny name, where everyone wants to live. In 2011, *New Jersey Monthly* magazine picked Ho-Ho-Kus as the number one place to live in the state of New Jersey. How did Ho-Ho-Kus get its name? Well, the origin is in dispute. Some say it was a Delaware Indian name for "red cedar." Others claim it was a Dutch idiom for "high oaks" or "high acorns." Regardless, it is a very nice place to live and a great place from which to commute to New York City, which is only about 25 miles away.

Four thousand people live within its 1.75 square-mile limits. With its proud Lenni Lenape Indian, Dutch, English, and Polish forbearers, Ho-Ho-Kus is a beautiful bedroom community with exceptional schools, fine dining, and a quiet Downtown area.

Ho-Ho-Kus has quite an exciting history. Some Revolutionary War buffs claim George Washington stayed at the Ho-Ho-Kus Inn, but all historians agree that Aaron Burr, the third vice president of the United States was married at the Hermitage in 1782, a Ho-Ho-Kus landmark. Whether you are raising a family, eating at a four-star restaurant, or antiquing in its famous shops, Ho-Ho-Kus, New Jersey, is hard to beat.

FRANKLIN LAKES

NEW JERSEY

The borough of Franklin Lakes is an affluent metropolitan suburb and a very desirable place to live and raise a family, especially for those who seek a great deal of privacy.

One of the major differences between Franklin Lakes and many of the neighboring towns in Bergen County is that it is less developed. The borough has a population of approximately 10,500 people, while the nearby village of Ridgewood, for example, which is considerably smaller in area, has a population of about 25,000 people.

Unless you live, work, or frequently visit the area, you would probably be surprised by how much wilderness remains in this eco-friendly community. Several residents with whom we spoke have seen black bears and coyotes on their properties, and sightings of bald eagles are not uncommon either.

One of the area's most popular spots for hiking, bird watching, and enjoying nature is the Franklin Lakes Nature Preserve, a 147-acre protected sanctuary that is open to the public. The preserve is especially popular with dog owners and fishermen. Visitors are allowed to bring dogs, as long as they are kept on their leash, and fishing is also permitted, as long as what is caught is released.

Another popular area where residents can enjoy nature as well as multiple recreational activities is the Indian Trail Club. The private club has spectacular facilities and is surrounded by a picturesque natural setting, which includes a large lake. Members enjoy a variety of activities ranging from fishing and sailing to tennis and swimming. During the winter, the sport of paddle tennis reigns supreme.

Finally, the town profile of Franklin Lakes would not be complete without a mention of the area's well known specialty grocery store, The Market Basket, which is perhaps the best place to do your food shopping anywhere in the tristate area.

Franklin Lakes Nature Preserve

THANK YOU FOR HELPING TO PROTECT OUR PARK
AND KEEP IT CLEAN

PARKING ENTRANCE ON HIGH MOUNTAIN ROAD

PARK RULES AND REGULATIONS

FISHING PERMITTED WITH NJ STATE LICENSE
PLEASE DO NOT LEAVE TRASH BEHIND (CARRY IN - CARRY OUT)
OPEN DAWN TO DUSK
NO LITTERING
NO BOATS, NO SWIMMING, NO WADING
NO MOTORIZED VEHICLES
NO ALCOHOL
NO FIRES
DOGS MUST BE KEPT ON LEASH
AND PLEASE PICK UP AFTER YOUR DOG

THE BOROUGH REQUESTS THAT FISHERMEN

CATCH AND RELEASE

AT THE FRANKLIN LAKES NATURE PRESERVE

CATCH &

RELEASE

THE CELERY FARMS

ALLENDALE, NEW JERSEY

The town of Allendale, located in Bergen County, New Jersey, made a fantastic investment for their residents when they bought the Celery Farm and turned it into a 110-acre, protected wildlife preserve. Today this beautiful oasis, located in the midst of an urban sprawl, is home to a surprisingly large number of plants and animals. Over 200 species of birds have been spotted in this nature preserve and the area has developed an incredibly loyal following among bird watchers. The Celery Farm is also home to a large number of mammals, including red fox and an occasional mink. The farm has also been known to be one of the few areas in northern New Jersey where you may catch a glimpse of the endangered wood turtle.

Animals are not the only ones who enjoy this wildlife area. The Celery Farm is popular for hikers, joggers, photographers, and, of course, hockey players. During the winter, when the pond freezes over, pond hockey is the main focus of most visitors. It should be noted that the Celery Farm is open to the public, but if you plan on playing pond hockey with the locals, make sure you bring your "A" game.

A special thanks to Dr. Jerry Barrack, the photographer who captured these wildlife images at the Celery Farm and allowed us to use them for this book.

A PLACE THAT TIME HAS FORGOTTEN

From exotic antique plants to rare Koi, Waterford Gardens provides an oasis of beauty and tranquility that is just a short drive from Manhattan.

WATERFORD GARDENS

SADDLE RIVER, NEW JERSEY

Waterford Gardens is a 95-year-old, family-owned aquaculture center, where water plants are grown for outdoor water gardens and ponds. It offers a wonderful opportunity for visitors to step back in time to see a business that has not changed much since the early 1900s.

John, David, and Katie Meeks, the sibling proprietors of Waterford Gardens, have kept this idyllic setting true to its rustic beginnings, which adds to its unique charm. Original concrete tanks, ten inches deep and 100 feet long, are filled with a great variety of plants, from exotic irises to night-blooming water lilies. Multicolored lotus plants fill one section, while floating bog plants fill another. Children will especially like the ubiquitous Paradise Fish, which were added to the tanks years ago to control uninvited mosquito larvae from hatching in this jungle-

like atmosphere. If your little ones put their hands in the water, these little tropical fish will nibble at their fingers.

Besides water plants, Waterford Gardens also offer a diverse variety of rare Japanese Koi and common pond goldfish. Prices range from a few dollars for common goldfish to several thousand dollars per fish for one-of-a-kind, show-winning Koi, as large as full-grown Striped Bass. Outdoor ponds surround the greenhouse complex, and there are food pellet dispensers so children can feed the huge, tame Koi, that will literally eat out of their hands.

After you have completed the inside tour and you finish feeding the fish, be sure to take a walk around the entire property. Wildlife sightings are common at Waterford Gardens, and don't be surprised if you see egrets, deer, hawks, giant bull frogs, water snakes, and several different types of turtles.

A Fish Tale

The magnificent orange and black bButterfly Koi pictured above is the most beautiful fish I have ever seen. Seeing this beloved pet and Waterford Gardens mascot was always one of the highlights during a trip to the garden center. The exceptionally long fins and striking pattern that cover this elegant fish are only part of the reason why this Koi was such a fan favorite among Waterford Gardens' enthusiasts. A friendly and gentle fish, this particular Koi would immediately swim right up to visitors and eat fish pellets out of their hands. Even longtime Koi breeders and savvy fish experts would be surprised by the incredibly friendly and charming personality of this unique fish.

The popularity and mystique of this fish was only enhanced after an unusual turn of events. Hurricane Floyd hit the Saddle River, New Jersey, area particularly hard, causing an enormous amount of flooding. A huge rainstorm ensued and caused the Saddle River, which runs beside the Waterford Gardens, to overflow and wash out many of the outdoor pond fish, including the massive orange and black butterfly Koi. After the storm, a local trout fisherman found the prize Koi in a deep pool a mile away and returned the fish to the Gardens. After his surprise return, the fish was given the name Floyd.

Unfortunately, Floyd was stolen in 2010 and the disturbing "fishnapping" story was featured in several newspapers and television news stories. To date, the crime remains unsolved. However, Floyd has already beaten the odds once and we do hope that one day he will be returned to his home at Waterford Gardens.

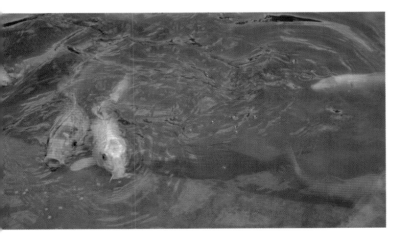

RAMAPO RESERVATION

MAHWAH, NEW JERSEY

The Ramapo Valley Reservation is a county park, open to the public, located in Mahwah, New Jersey. With over 3,000 acres of dense forests, open fields, swamps, mountain-like terrain, ponds, the Ramapo River, and a mountain brook with a waterfall, the park has a loyal following of hikers, trail runners, and fishermen.

One of the most popular destinations at the reservation is an area referred to as "Unemployment Rock." There is a marked trail that brings you to the top of a mountainous incline, leading to a stunning lake. Once at the lake if you bear right, follow the trail for about a quarter mile, until you arrive at a large area of

flat rocks on a mild incline. This picturesque area has attracted swimmers and sunbathers for generations. It got its nickname many years ago, due to the fact that it was usually crowded not only on weekends but also during the week, the majority of the crowd being teenagers and unemployed young adults.

Despite the heavy foot traffic, the Ramapo Reservation is actually a great place to observe wildlife. Copperheads, rattlesnakes and black bears have all been seen at the reservation, so it might be a good idea to stay on the marked trails during your visit.

TIMBER RATTLESNAKES &
NORTHERN COPPERHEADS
may be found in this area.

They are important members of
the natural community and they
are protected by law.⁺ They do
not attack but will defend
themselves if disturbed or
cornered.

GIVE THEM DISTANCE AND RESPECT

✚ NJ Endangered & Nongame Species Conservation Act
(NJSA 23:2A-1-13)

FAR HILLS
RACE MEETING

FAR HILLS, NEW JERSEY

Each fall, more than 35,000 spectators come to Moorland Farm in Far Hills, New Jersey, for the state's biggest social event of the fall season, The Far Hills Race Meeting. October 20, 2012, marked the 92nd year of this annual tradition and featured some of the world's finest steeplechase horses competing against the stunning backdrop of New Jersey's fall foliage.

The Far Hills Race Meeting is a unique mix of society and sport, and features top thoroughbred jump racing, individualized tailgating parties, and culinary feasts. The event traces its origins to the Essex Hunt, a fox hunting event founded in 1870. Since the 1950s, it has raised more than $18 million to benefit Somerset Medical Center.

The Far Hills Race Meeting is truly a community event where you are just as likely to see families playing around the hay bales as you are to see racing fans cheering on their favorite horses. At the 2012 race, over fifty of the finest thoroughbreds on the National Steeplechase Association circuit traveled from across the country to compete in the event's six races. Purses ranged from $25,000 to $250,000, the largest of any steeplechase race in the country.

In addition to the races, lavish, personalized tailgating parties are a highlight of the overall experience and often have imaginative themes and food. The race serves as a great place to reconnect and celebrate with family and friends, and has become an annual tradition for many spectators, with some groups coming to the event since the 1950s.

FAR HILLS RACE MEETING ASSOCIATION

RUMSON

NEW JERSEY

Originally a summer retreat for wealthy New York City bankers and titans of industry, today the town of Rumson has become a thriving, year-round community that offers the townsfolk the best of everything. Located in Monmouth County, New Jersey, the community was built on a picturesque peninsula overlooking the ocean. The town is also bound by the Navesink River and the Shrewsberry River.

Adding to the natural beauty of Rumson are many of the spectacular, turn-of-the-century estates that were built along the shores of both rivers. Surprisingly, many have remained intact and are just as beautiful now as they were when they were first built, over a hundred years ago. Hats off to the residents who have maintained and restored these antique homes, and kept their stunning gardens meticulously tended. Because of the preservation of these historic estates, the town has retained its character, charm, and much of the natural beauty for which it was originally known.

Besides being a picture-perfect town, it also happens to be an exciting place to live. With the ocean and two rivers in their backyard, locals enjoy water activities including everything from sailing and surfing to crabbing and clamming. If you happen to be a nature lover, you are in luck, as blue herons, egrets, osprey, red foxes, and hawks can be seen on a fairly regular basis.

Great schools, fantastic restaurants, one of the nation's most prestigious private tennis clubs, and an incredible shopping district just five minutes away in nearby Red Bank are a few reasons why Rumson continues to be a great place to live.

SPRING LAKE

NEW JERSEY

One of the most spectacular oceanfront communities in the tristate area is Spring Lake, New Jersey, known affectionately by locals as the Irish Riviera, a moniker undoubtedly related to the large number of residents claiming Irish ancestry. Once a summer-only retreat for the well-to-do from New York City and Philadelphia, Spring Lake has evolved into a mostly year-round community of 3,500 that doubles in size from its tiny population every summer.

Spring Lake is named for the spring-fed lake in the center of town. The town is bordered on the north by Lake Como, the south by the tidal Wreck Pond, which is great for crabbing, and on the east by the shimmering Atlantic Ocean. It has a total landmass of under two square miles.

The nearly two-mile-long, non-commercial boardwalk and two saltwater pools on the north and south end of the boardwalk are certainly part of the town's undeniable allure.

Stunning waterfront homes, a charming shopping district, great fishing, both saltwater and fresh, beautiful beaches, remarkable surfing, and an incredible private tennis club overlooking the ocean are a few more reasons why Spring Lake is a popular spot for both locals and summer visitors.

Many of the local families are fourth generation Spring Lakers, and a majority of young adults who grow up there return as soon as they can afford the cost of re-entry.

For weekend visitors looking to explore this charming town, there are a number of hotels and bed-and-breakfasts, including the Chateau Inn & Suites, one of the best hotels along the Jersey Shore.

The Black Swan

During the summer, my parents vacationed in Spring Lake, New Jersey. Their beach house is across the street from a protected wetlands area called Wreck Pond. The area is home to an abundance of wildlife and is a popular spot to go crabbing and fishing. Over the years we have been fortunate to have had some great sightings at Wreck Pond, but nothing can compare with the appearance of a magnificent black swan that I witnessed during the summer of 2009.

Early one morning, during the first week of July 2009, I received a phone call from my father urging me to drop everything and drive down to Spring Lake immediately. He was certain that he had seen a black swan swimming in Wreck Pond. He insisted that I come down to take pictures. Although I was somewhat skeptical I drove down from Ridgewood, New Jersey to take a look for myself.

When I got there, it was still early and most of Wreck Pond was covered with fog and mist. I waited patiently hoping to catch a glimpse of the majestic creature. Suddenly, out of the mist, a group of six swans began swimming towards me. I couldn't believe what I was seeing; it looked like one of the swans was, in fact, black. The swans swam past me, giving me a great opportunity to photograph them. For a split second, it seemed as though they were posing for me.

After working as a photographer for over ten years, I can say without hesitation that this is my favorite photograph that I have ever taken. I am glad I listened to my father's advice and drove down to Spring Lake that morning.

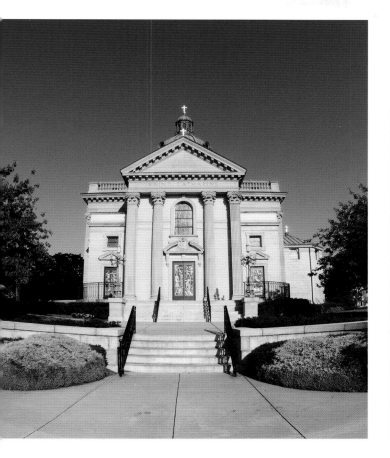

SEA GIRT

NEW JERSEY

Sea Girt, is a beautiful, ocean-front resort, located about 65 miles south of New York City. It is small, 1.5 square miles, but has over a mile of ocean frontage. Formerly a farm, Sea Girt was transformed into a classic beach town in the late 1800s. One hundred twenty acres of this tiny enclave were carved out in 1887 to make a New Jersey National Guard training facility that has been used continuously since the Spanish American War. This facility generously shares its open space with local baseball and lacrosse programs.

The town of Sea Girt also is home to the last shore lighthouse with a keeper's residence to be built on the East Coast of the United States. It still stands and is used for art shows and other community activities.

Sea Girt boasts a year-round boardwalk overlooking its large beach and the Atlantic Ocean. It always seems to be busy and it is a favorite meeting place for residents and visitors.

When visiting this charming Victorian community, be sure to have lunch or dinner at the famous Parker House, a massive three-story, all-wood restaurant that has been feeding the masses for 134 years. But get there early, because there is always a line and everyone wants to eat on the massive porches.

BAY HEAD

NEW JERSEY

Bay Head, New Jersey, is known as a country village by the sea. It is a Victorian postcard located on the Atlantic Ocean. While it is very tiny, being less than 0.70 square miles in size, with a population under 1,000, it is one of the most desirable locations for summer folk.

While all the beaches are public, with strategic access in various locations, it is virtually "for residents only" as the town has almost no parking or restroom facilities for visitors. Still that doesn't seem to affect the allure that Bay Head has for summer visitors.

While Bay Head is located on the Atlantic Ocean, part of it is on the head of Barnegat Bay and it is because of this auspicious location that it was so named Bay Head by railroad men labeling that train stop in the 1880s. Bay Head is known mostly as a treasured "shore town," untouched by time, and with 4th and 5th generation families and pristine beaches.

You know that you have arrived as a resident if you belong to the storied Bay Head Yacht Club. Located on the bay, it has beautiful tennis courts, docking for club members' vessels, and a great dining hall surrounded by boat flags from far and near. The Club even has its own Commodore and has memorable Memorial Day, Fourth of July and Labor Day parties that are wonderful to attend and truly something to see. If you are one of the lucky 1,000 residents, then you are truly fortunate, as this is one of the most sought out locations on New Jersey's Gold Coast.

SUBURBAN CLASSIC GALS

Without the help of the young ladies pictured here, and countless others who helped over the years, there would never have been a magazine *Suburban Classic*. Quite frankly, without the magazine there would never have been a book. *Suburban Classic* hired dozens of high school and college students to take our publication and canvas the neighborhoods of Fairfield County, Connecticut, Bergen County, New Jersey, Westchester, New York, the Gold Coast of Long Island, and the Hamptons. Not only did the girls help get *Suburban Classic* much needed publicity, they also provided numerous suggestions for potential stories that would be of interest to our readers. As the magazine grew, so did the responsibility of many of our young employees.

Several of the girls graduated to high level positions and were soon writing stories, editing photos, and securing interviews with well-known architects, builders, writers, and successful entrepreneurs. The most important contribution the girls made, however, was their ability to go out and sell subscriptions. By getting their friends and family to subscribe, it allowed our small group of employees to spend their time being creative and developing stories with unique content.

A very special thanks for the young ladies who helped make both the magazine and book possible. The enthusiasm and effort they put forth is truly appreciated.

ACKNOWLEDGMENTS

I wish to thank the following people for contributing to this book:

To Dan Burns, photographer extraordinaire who accompanied me on countless photo shoots and who provided both the magazine and this book with some truly spectacular images. Dan is one of the most talented and dedicated photographers I have ever met and without his contribution the book would not look the same.

To Steve Turner, the best aerial photographer in the business. Steve took almost all of the aerial photographs that appear in the book, including the cover.

To Jackie Boswick, a longtime employee of Summer Heatt who has helped coach hundreds of lacrosse clinics and camps over the past six years. I have known Jackie since she was 10 years old from when she played lacrosse in our local camps and clinics. Now a college student and studying design, she offered to help with the book and worked tirelessly for over a year by editing photos, arranging interviews, and preparing the book to be submitted in an acceptable design. Without her help, the book may not have been completed on time, if at all.

To Meredith McBride and Ryerson Kipp, the most talented artists I have ever worked with. This husband and wife team transformed our magazine after the first issue came out and they gave *Suburban Classic* a more polished and elegant look. Without their help there never would have been a second issue of *Suburban Classic* magazine and there certainly never would have been a book.

To Cindy Rinfret, the worlds greatest interior designer and one of the very few people to support Suburban Classic right from the start. Cindy introduced me to everybody, got me interviews with celebrities, and prominently displayed every issue of our magazine in her beautiful home and garden store on Greenwich Avenue.

To Kerri MacKay and Tara Ciriello for being my typist, proofreaders, critics, and advisors.

To The Kaali-Nagy Company for providing dozens of exquisite high quality photos of their residential creations, which we were allowed to include in our magazine and in this book. Many of the homes featured in the Greenwich, Darien, and New Canaan sections of this book were designed and built by the Kaali-Nagy Company.

To the Robinson brothers: Richards, Stephen and Peter for their loyalty and support.

To Valerie Donohue, the photographer who captured the amazing wildlife images at the Rye Marshland Conservancy and allowed us to use them in this book.

To Dr. Jerry Barrack, who provided us with some truly spectacular photos of the Celery Farms in Allendale, NJ, and allowed us to use them in this book.

To Brooke Perry, who wrote dozens of articles for *Suburban Classic* magazine and encouraged me to write this book.

To Mark and Cathy Mariani, for always allowing us to display *Suburban Classic* magazine at their beautiful garden center and of course for helping me get the perfect cover shot.

To the Far Hills Racing Association for all their help.

To my younger brother and best friend Joe Jackson – the only person in this world that I have ever trusted. At 23 years old I won a small lawsuit settlement. I was planning on buying a convertible. My brother convinced me to instead take the money and go into business with him and start Summer Heatt. Today, 17 years later, Summer Heatt Sports is one of the largest and most successful youth sports organizations on the east coast. Over 12,000 children participate annually in Connecticut, New York, and New Jersey. If I hadn't taken my brother's advice I would not have had the opportunity to be doing what I am doing today, which is coaching lacrosse, writing, and working as a photographer.

Finally, I would like to thank those talented people, without whom this book would not have been completed.